The wind that blows is
ALL THAT
ANYBODY KNOWS

The wind that blows is
ALL THAT
ANYBODY KNOWS

the thoughts of

Henry David Thoreau

edited and with an introduction by

Rod McKuen

photographs by

Helen Miljakovich

STANYAN BOOKS

RANDOM HOUSE

A Stanyan book published by Stanyan Books,
8721 Sunset Blvd., Los Angeles, California,
and, by Random House, Inc.,
201 E. 50th St., New York, N.Y.

Printed in the United States of America

Design / Anthony Goldschmidt

For Jack Coates

THOREAU
an appreciation by ROD McKUEN

Henry David Thoreau dropped out. Not where he would take up air and space that other people paid for and give them nothing in return. He went away to Walden Pond to be alone, to work alone, to rethink his life. He was to live for a time in the world of animals and birds and God. Coming back into a world of people he brought with him writings that could have been set down yesterday.

Thoreau learned of people by living without them. He traded city summers for the green of trees and the green of hills. He gave up year upon year of comfortable fires in winter for the quiet cold of the country. People's faces were replaced by anything and everything but people's faces.

If rivers come out of their icy prison thus bright and immortal, shall not I too resume my spring life with joy and hope? Have I not hope to sparkle on the spring of life's current?

In reality Henry Thoreau gave up nothing and gained everything. His most important acquisition being his new self.

We are near to being passengers on his trip to Walden because Thoreau was as near to being every man of conscience and of care as any man before him or after him has been or was.

Only those mechanics he could work out for himself, only those lives he could enrich or those who could enrich his own, only the truths he knew to be true interested him or made sense to him. It should be so with all of us. If it ever is, Henry David Thoreau will cease to be a wise man for he will be a common man. He would surely have liked that.

Rod McKuen / December 1969

Man and his surroundings

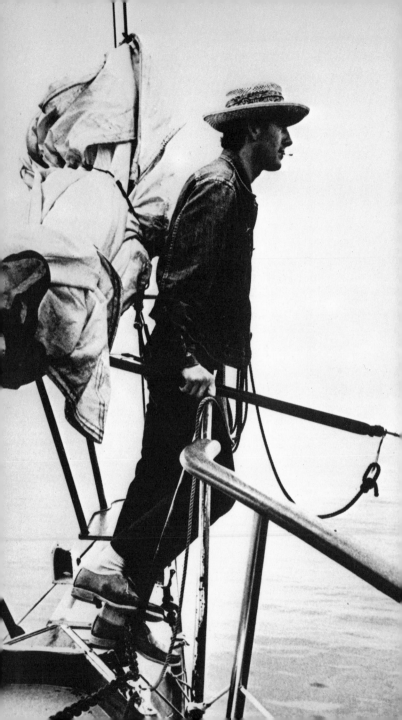

What a man thinks of himself, that is which determines, or rather indicates his fate.

The mass of men lead lives of quiet desperation. What is called resignation is confirmed desperation. From the desperate city you go into the desperate country, and have to console yourself with the bravery of minks and muskrats. A stereotyped but unconscious despair is concealed even under what are called the games and amusements of mankind. There is no play in them, for this comes after work. But it is a characteristic of wisdom not to do desperate things.

When we consider what, to use the words of the catechism, is the chief end of man, and what are the true necessaries and means of life, it appears as if men had deliberately chosen the common mode of living because they preferred it to any other. Yet they honestly think there is no choice left. But alert and healthy natures remember that the sun rose clear.

It is never too late to give up our prejudices. No way of thinking or doing, however ancient, can be trusted without proof. What everybody echoes or in silence passes by as true today may turn out to be falsehood tomorrow, mere smoke of opinion, which some had trusted for a cloud that would sprinkle fertilizing rain on their fields.

If a man does not keep pace with his companions, perhaps it is because he hears a different drummer. Let him step to the music which he hears, however measured or far away.

A man thinking or working is not always alone. Let him be where he will.

It is not necessary that a man should earn his living by the sweat of his brow, unless he sweats easier than I do.

Heaven might be defined as the place which men avoid.

Any man more right than his neighbor constitutes a majority of one.

The man who goes alone can start today, but he who travels with another must wait till that other is ready.

Men will lie on their backs, talking about the fall of man, and never make an effort to get up.

All that man has to say or do that can possibly concern mankind is in some shape or other to tell the story of his love—to sing, and, if he is fortunate and keeps alive, he will be forever in love.

Men have become the tools of their tools. The man who independently plucked the fruits when he was hungry is become a farmer; and he who stood under a tree for shelter, a housekeeper. We now no longer camp as for a night, but have settled down on earth and forgotten heaven.

We have built for this world a family mansion, and the next a family tomb. The best works of art are the expression of man's struggle to free himself from this condition, but the effect of our art is merely to make this low state comfortable and that higher state to be forgotten. There is actually no place in this village for a work of *fine* art, if any had come down to us, to stand, for our lives, our houses and streets, furnish no proper pedestal for it.

Most men, even in this comparatively free country, through mere ignorance and mistake, are so occupied with the factitious cares and superfluously coarse labors of life that its finer fruits cannot be plucked by them. Their fingers, from excessive toil, are too clumsy and tremble too much for that. Actually, the laboring man has not leisure for a true integrity day by day; he cannot afford to sustain the manliest relations to men; his labor would be depreciated in the market. He has no time to be anything but a machine.

The most I can do for my friend is simply to be his friend.

To be awake

is to be alive.

We are all sculptures and painters

and our material is our own flesh and blood and bones.

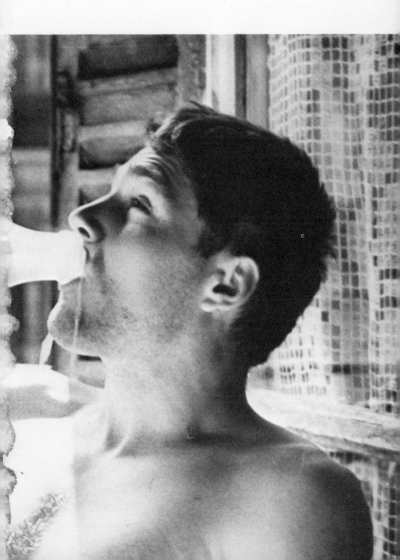

When I hear a grown man or woman say, "Once I had faith in men, now I have not," I am inclined to ask, "Who are you whom the world has disappointed? Have not you rather disappointed the world?"

Let us have noble villages of men. If it is necessary, omit one bridge over the river, go round a little there, and throw one arch at least over the darker gulf of ignorance which surrounds us.

While civilization has been improving our houses, it has not equally improved the men who are to inhabit them...

I think that we are not commonly aware that man is our contemporary—that in this strange, outlandish world, so barren, so prosaic, fit not to live in but merely to pass through, that even here so divine a creature as man does actually live.

The youth gets together his materials to build a bridge to the moon, or, perchance, a palace or temple on the earth, and, at length, the middle-aged man concludes to build a wood-shed with them.

Heaven
is under
our feet
as well
as over
our heads.

wisdom...
and the wonders of God and nature.

Motions everywhere in nature must surely be the circulations of God. The flowing sail, the running stream, the waving tree, the roving wind—whence else their infinite health and freedom. I can see nothing so proper and holy as unrelaxed play and frolic in this bower God has built for us.

Knowledge does not come to us by details, but in flashes of light from heaven.

None can be an impartial or wise observer of human life but from the vantage ground of what we should call voluntary poverty.

One generation abandons the enterprises of another like stranded vessels.

God did not make this world in jest; no, nor in indifference.

In accumulating property for ourselves or our posterity, in founding a family or a state, or acquiring fame even, we are mortal; but in dealing with truth we are immortal, and need fear no change nor accident.

The highest condition of art is artlessness.

If misery loves company, misery has company enough.

I never found the companion that was so companionable as solitude. We are for the most part more lonely when we go abroad among men than when we stay in our chambers. A man thinking or working is always alone, let him be where he will.

Blessed are they who never read a newspaper, for they shall see Nature, and, through her, God.

We do not ride on the railroad; it rides upon us.

In a pleasant spring morning all men's sins are forgiven. Through our own recovered innocence we discern the innocence of our neighbors.

The right of revolution...

There will never be a really free and enlightened state, until the state comes to recognize the individual as a higher and independent power, from which all its own power and authority are derived, and treats him accordingly. I please myself with imagining a state at last which can afford to be just to all men, and to treat the individual with respect as a neighbor; which even would not think it inconsistent with its own repose, if a few were to live aloof from it, not meddling with it, nor embraced by it, who fulfilled at the duties of neighbors and fellowmen. A state which bore this kind of fruit, and suffered it to drop off as fast as it ripened, would prepare the way for a still more perfect and glorious state, which also I have imagined, but not yet anywhere seen.

All men recognize the right of revolution; that is, the right to refuse allegiance to and to resist the government, when its tyranny or its inefficiency are great and unendurable.

A government in which the majority rule in all cases cannot be based on justice even as far as men are concerned.

I heartily accept the motto — "That government is best which governs least;" and I should like to see it acted up to more rapidly and systematically. Carried out, it finally amounts to this, which also I believe — "That government is best which governs not at all;" and when men are prepared for it, that will be the kind of government which they will have.

Let every man make known what kind of government would command his respect and that will be one step toward obtaining it.

Unjust laws exist; shall we be content to obey them, or shall we endeavor to amend them, and obey them until we have succeeded, or shall we transgress them at once? Men generally, under such a government as this, think that they ought to wait until they have persuaded the majority to alter them. They think that, if they should resist, the remedy would be worse than the evil. It makes it worse.

Why is it not more apt to anticipate and provide for reform?

Why does it not cherish its wise minority?

Why does it cry and resist before it is hurt?

Why does it not encourage its citizens to be on the alert to point out its faults, and *do* better than it would have them?

We believe that the possibility of the future far exceeds the accomplishment of the past. We review the past with the common sense, but we anticipate the future with transcendental senses. In our sanest moments we find ourselves naturally expecting or prepared for far greater changes than any which we have experienced within the period of distinct memory, only to be paralleled by experiences which are forgotten. Perchance there are revolutions which create an interval impassable to the memory.

to think about.

1. Beware of all enterprises that require new clothes, and not rather a new wearer of clothes.

2. Let your affairs be as two or three, and not a hundred.

3. Keep three chairs in your house. One for solitude, two for friendship, three for society.

4. To preserve your relationship to nature, make your life more moral, more pure, more innocent.